Jimmy's Goal

Written by Sandra Iversen
Illustrated by Pat Reynolds

Jimmy plays soccer.
Today is his first big game.
Jimmy's mom is watching.

Jimmy has some new black shoes.
He has some new blue shorts
and a new red shirt.

Jimmy is the goal keeper.
He has to keep the ball
out of the net.
Jimmy watches the ball
all the time.

The boys and girls
on Jimmy's team
kick the ball to each other.
Big Pete bounces the ball
off his head.

The ball goes into the net.
Jimmy's team has
scored a goal.
"Great!" yell the moms and dads.

Jimmy watches the ball.
The boys and girls
are kicking the ball.
The boys and girls
are kicking the ball
toward Jimmy.

Jimmy watches the ball.
It comes toward him.
He bounces it off his head
just like Big Pete.
The ball goes into the net.

"Oh, no!" moan the moms and dads.
"Jimmy has scored a goal.
But Jimmy has put the ball
in the wrong net!"